GIVE YOUR
FAITH AN ASSIGNMENT

BISHOP ANDREW MERRITT

A & V Publishing Company
Southfield, MI 48034

ISBN: 978-0-9637640-7-2

Printed in the United States of America.

A Practical Guide

Understand the concepts of faith and how to apply your faith to obtain God-given promises.

Best-selling Author
Andrew J.D. Merritt

Other Books Authored By Andrew J.D. Merritt

Travel Prayers: How to Pray for Safe Travel

My Faith is Taking Me Someplace

Expectation: Are You Positioned to Receive Your Victory?

Jesus Destroyed the Works of the Devil

Pursue, Overtake, and Reclaim

The Marriage Enrichment Handbook

If you want to learn more about Andrew J.D. Merritt, his ministry, books, CDs or music catalog, please go to **bishopmerritt.org** or call 313.491.8430.

DEDICATION

This book is dedicated to all my loving grandchildren...

Haki Turner, Kirkland Williams II, Mariah Greathouse, Lorne Bowman II, Aaron (Drew) Bowman, Ryan Everett, Lillian Merritt, Josiah Everett, Cristina Merritt, Andrew Merritt II, and Alexandria Merritt.

And to all my future generations to come.

"The counsel of the Lord stands forever, the plans of His heart to all generations."

(Psalm 33:11 NKJV)

Faith

"Now faith is the assurance (title deed, confirmation) of things hoped for (divinely guaranteed), and the evidence of things not seen [the conviction of their reality—faith comprehends as fact what cannot be experienced by the physical senses]."

(Hebrews 11:1 AMP)

ACKNOWLEDGMENTS

In every author's life, thoughts, concepts and ideas are revealed. But unless someone can assist him or her in presenting God's heart on paper— they are never revealed to the world.

I have found such a one in Dr. Cynthia Marks. God Bless you and His face forever shine upon you and may His riches and best always be yours.

Bishop Andrew JD Merritt

CONTENTS

INTRODUCTION

Faith Is Not Just A Word;
Faith Is An Action *Because* Of
A Word From God

Writing a book on **Giving Your Faith An Assignment** is the zenith of over forty years of using my God-given faith to obtain the promises that God has purposed for my life.

As a nationally renowned pastor, my life has been an open book. My family, congregation and countless others have witnessed first-hand how I have decreed a thing based on a rhema word from God. Then I began to step out in faith and ultimately walked into God's best.

These concepts are not some New Age "see it and believe it." No! I am sharing Bible-based principles used by other great men of faith, such as Abraham.

In Genesis 13:14-17 (KJV) we read:

*And the LORD said unto Abram, after that Lot was separated from him, **Lift up now thine eyes**, **and look** from the place where thou art northward, and southward, and eastward, and westward:*

*For all the land which thou seest, to thee will I give it, and to thy seed for ever. And I will make thy seed as the dust of the earth: so that if a man can number the dust of the earth, then shall thy seed also be numbered. **Arise, walk through the land** in the length of it and in the breadth of it; for I will give it unto thee.*

Abram heard a rhema word from God. He acted upon it and received.

As you read, study and apply these teachings in your life consistently, you too will experience the manifestation of your faith assignment.

WHEN DID HAVING FAITH BECOME IMPORTANT?

Many critics of "faith teaching" feel that it is a fad or a new thing that preachers came up with just to "get the peoples' money." Many will cite that the teaching on having faith started with Kenneth E. Hagin, Sr. who is often referred to as the "father" or the pioneer of the Word of Faith movement.

Let us take a moment to consider some important facts:

- The word **faith** (or a derivative) appears in the *King James Version* of the Bible 338 times![1]
- The first **KJV** was printed 1611.

---

[1] http://www.kingjamesbibleonline.org

- Historical records show that the original Hebrew manuscripts that make up the 39 books of the Old Testament and the Septuagint Greek manuscripts, which contain the 39 Old Testament books and 14 Apocrypha books were completed in 500 BC and 200 BC respectively.
- Hagin begin as an itinerant ministry Bible teacher and evangelist in 1949.

Therefore, it is obvious that teaching about faith did not have its genesis with Brother Hagin. So the question begs, when did this emphasis on faith begin?

Genesis 15:6 KJV says,

*And he **believed** in the LORD; and he counted it to him for righteousness.*

This Scripture is talking about Abram who later became Abraham. Why? Because of his belief or faith in what God said in **Genesis 15:5-7**.

The New Testament, **Romans 4:16** tells us that it is Abraham who is the "father of faith":

*For Abraham is the father of all who believe (**NLT**).*

When Did Having Faith Become Important?

...the fulfillment of God's promise depends entirely on trusting God and his way, and then simply embracing him and what he does. God's promise arrives as pure gift. That's the only way everyone can be sure to get in on it... He is our faith father (**Message**).

Furthermore, verse **18** (**Message**) reads: *When **everything** was hopeless, Abraham **believed** anyway, deciding to live not on the basis of what he saw he couldn't do but on what God said he would do.*

The word "believed" in this verse is *aman*, which means: To be firm, established and steady. It is translated with other words such as: believe, assurance, faithful, sure, trust, verified, steadfast.[2] This word is a

> *Abraham is the father of faith because when everything was hopeless, he decided not to live on what he could do, but decided to say AMEN to the promises of GOD!*

derivative of the familiar word "AMEN" that means: so be it or I agree it is true!

---

[2] Strong's Concordance Hebrew aman # 539

Students and preachers of the Bible often refer to the principle called the "**The Law of First Mention**," which means *the very first time any important word is mentioned in the Bible.*

So the **first mention** of faith is in the **first book** of the Bible.

It is recorded that Abram lived approximately 1800-2000 years before Jesus Christ. Could it be that from the very beginning God was rewarding those who firmly trusted and had confidence in what He had promised?

> *When God wanted to guarantee His promises, He gave His word, a rock-solid guarantee.*
>
> *God can't break His word.*
>
> *And because His word cannot change, the promise is likewise unchangeable.*
>
> **Hebrews 6:17-18**
> **Message**

In the contemporary church, we have all heard countless sermons and read numerous books about faith. In fact, as of this writing, Amazon has almost 150,000 books on the topic of Christian faith. So it is obvious there is no lack of information on the subject. However, there is a lack of manifestation of the *faith* that we know so much about. The problem is not with God. The real problem is that we have a lot of information, but we do not know how to make correct application of what we know. And with incorrect application of faith there is no corresponding manifestation. If you have been exercising your faith and not seeing any sustainable evidence, then this is the book that you have been waiting for. This is your God-inspired guide to **Give Your Faith An Assignment**!

WHAT'S IN IT FOR ME?

Several sources suggest there are over 5000 promises in the Bible.[3] The promises of God are the will of God for His children.

Dear friends, now we are God's children…

1 John 3:2, GOD'S WORD TRANSLATION

The word promise is defined by **Baker's Evangelical Dictionary of Biblical Theology** [4] as "the assurance that one will or will not undertake a certain action." The **Merriam-Webster**

---

[3]http://www.family-times.net
There are approximately 8,810 promises in the entire Bible. In the Old Testament there are 7,706, and in the New Testament there are 1,104 wonderful promises. Deuteronomy 28 has 133 promises, which is more than any other chapter in the Bible.
http://www.goodnewsdispatch.org/promises.html
Throughout His Word, God makes a lot of promises to believers! How many promises are there? As many as 7,000.

[4] www.studylight.org/dic/bed

Dictionary[5] defines a promise as "a legally binding declaration that gives the person to whom it is made a right to expect or to claim the performance or forbearance of a specified act."

God is not a man, so he does not lie.
He is not human, so he does not change his mind.
Has he ever spoken and failed to act?
Has he ever promised and not carried it through?
Numbers 23:19, New Living Translation

Unfortunately, because of their own life experiences, some people have a very poor image of fathers. Although many of us have had great fathers or have made great strides to be positive role models for our children, we would not have

> *If you then, who are evil, (imperfect, moral beings) know how to give good gifts to your children, how much more will your Father who is in heaven give good things to those who ask him!*
>
> **Matthew 7:11, ESV**

to go far to find people who would describe their fathers as absentee, untrustworthy, or a deadbeat.

---

[5] www.merriam-webster.com/dictionary/promise

However, that is not so with God. God our Father loves us with an everlasting love. He has promised to never leave or forsake us; He said His thoughts towards us are only good and even the more, He has promised to give us good gifts!

True, there are thousands promises in the Bible, but not every one of these promises applies to every single person. Some of the promises are just for the children of Israel (Jews), some are just for a specific person or for a specific period of time and some are for the Body of Christ (the Church). Let's look at examples of these different types of promises.

The promise made to Abraham and Sarah about having a son was *specifically* for them and was to manifest at a *specific* time.

Is anything impossible for the LORD? At the time set for it, I will return to you—about a year from now— and Sarah will have a son."

Genesis 18:14, International Standard Version

Whereas **Hebrews 13:5** contains a promised guarantee *to all* Christians: ...*Be happy with what* *you have because God has said, "I will never abandon you or leave you."*

GOD'S WORD TRANSLATION

And there is a precious promise that is *for all* sinners—Jew or Gentile:

For "everyone who calls on the name of the Lord will be saved."

Romans 10:13, ESV

Taking matters a bit further, the Bible shows us there two kinds of promises. One is an unconditional promise; the other is conditional. An example of the unconditional promise is Consider **Genesis 9:8-16**. In this text, God makes an unconditional promise that He will *never* again destroy the whole earth by means of a world-wide flood.

God also said to Noah and his sons,

I am going to make my promise to you, your descendants, and every living being that is with you-birds, domestic animals, and all the wild animals, all those that came out of the ship-every living thing on earth. I am making my promise to you. Never again will all life be killed by floodwaters. Never again will there be a flood that destroys the earth. God said, This is the sign of the promise I am giving to you and every living being that is with you for generations to come. I will put my rainbow in the clouds to be a sign of my promise to the earth. Whenever I form clouds over the earth, a rainbow will appear in the clouds. Then I will remember my promise to you and every living animal. Never again will water become a flood to destroy all life.

Whenever the rainbow appears in the clouds, I will see it and remember my everlasting promise to every living animal on earth.

GOD'S WORD TRANSLATION

No matter what men do or do not do, God made a promise that there would never again be another earth-destroying flood like the one found in **Genesis 6-8**. God did not put any conditions ("...if you will do this, then I will do that..."); the promise is unconditional.

It does not matter if men do the right kinds of things; if men do all the wrong kinds of things; if men believe the promise; or if men do not believe the promise. Unconditional promises are God's declaration of His commitment to honor His Word no matter what!

An example of a conditional promise is found in Deuteronomy 28:1-14:

The Blessings of Obedience

*And it shall come to pass, **if** thou shalt hearken diligently unto the voice of the LORD thy God, to observe and to do all his commandments which I command thee this day, that the LORD thy God will set thee on high above all nations of the earth:*

*And all these blessings shall come on thee, and overtake thee, **if** thou shalt hearken unto the voice of the LORD thy God.*

Blessed shalt thou be in the city, and blessed shalt thou be in the field.

Blessed shall be the fruit of thy body, and the fruit of thy ground, and the fruit of thy cattle, the increase of thy kine, and the flocks of thy sheep.

Blessed shall be thy basket and thy store.

Blessed shalt thou be when thou comest in, and blessed shalt thou be when thou goest out.

What's In It For Me?

The LORD shall cause thine enemies that rise up against thee to be smitten before thy face: they shall come out against thee one way, and flee before thee seven ways.

The LORD shall command the blessing upon thee in thy storehouses, and in all that thou settest thine hand unto; and he shall bless thee in the land which the LORD thy God giveth thee.

The LORD shall establish thee an holy people unto himself, as he hath sworn unto thee, if thou shalt keep the commandments of the LORD thy God, and walk in his ways.

And all people of the earth shall see that thou art called by the name of the LORD; and they shall be afraid of thee.

And the LORD shall make thee plenteous in goods, in the fruit of thy body, and in the fruit of thy cattle, and in the fruit of thy ground, in the land which the LORD sware unto thy fathers to give thee.

The LORD shall open unto thee his good treasure, the heaven to give the rain unto thy land in his season, and to bless all the work of thine hand: and thou shalt lend unto many nations, and thou shalt not borrow.

*And the LORD shall make thee the head, and not the tail; and thou shalt be above only, and thou shalt not be beneath; **if** that thou hearken unto the commandments of the LORD thy God, which I command thee this day, to observe and to do them:*

And thou shalt not go aside from any of the words which I command thee this day, to the right hand, or to the left, to go after other gods to serve them.

This Scripture has a *condition* attached to receiving the promise.

If we do what God requires as the condition, we shall receive what He has promised to do in response. In this instance the *condition* is obedience. The **NIV** translation of verses **1** and **2** make it clear:

> **Condition:**
> *A premise upon which the fulfillment of an agreement depends; a stipulation; a prerequisite; a restricting or modifying factor: a qualification*
>
> **Merriam-Webster Dictionary**

If you fully obey the Lord your God and carefully follow all his commands I give you today, the Lord your God will set you high above all the nations on *earth. All these blessings will come on you and accompany you **if you obey** the Lord your God.*

The Curses for Disobedience

*However, **if you do not obey** the Lord your God and do not carefully follow all his commands and decrees I am giving you today, all these curses will come on you and overtake you—* **Deuteronomy 28:15 (NIV)**

Another **conditional** promise is the promise of salvation. Yes it is God's desire that all should be saved and that none should perish or go to hell; however, this is based on the **condition** that we have to confess Jesus Christ as our Savior. This is indicated in multiple scriptures:

Whosoever therefore shall confess (acknowledge) me before men, him will I confess also before my Father which is in heaven.
Matthew 10:32 (KJV)

And it shall come to pass, that whosoever shall call on the name of the Lord shall be saved.
Acts 2:21 (KJV)

For whosoever shall call upon the name of the Lord shall be saved.
Romans 10:13 (KJV)

Finally, let's look at another aspect of the promises in the Bible, that being a **logos** word verses a **rhema** word. God's promises are in the Word of God; they are His promises to us as recorded by the inspiration of the Holy Spirit. Looking for the promises of God? Go to His Word!

> *"You can't sow, or praise or sing and dance your way out of disobedience. The Scripture is clear: you must be willing and obedient to receive the promises of God.*
> *You don't have to understand it — just do it."*
>
> **Bishop Andrew JD Merritt**

There are two Greek words that describe Scripture as they are translated in the New Testament. The first word, **logos**, refers primarily to the total inspired Word of God and to the person Jesus — Who is the living **Logos**.[6]

---

[6] Strong's Concordance Greek logos # 3056

The following passages of Scripture give biblical examples of the **logos** of God:

> *The seed is the word (**logos**) of God.* **Luke 8:11 (KJV)**
>
> *In the beginning was the Word (**logos**), and the Word (**logos**) was with God, and the Word (**logos**) was God.* **John 1:1 (KJV)**
>
> - *Study to show thyself approved unto God, a workman that needeth not to be ashamed, rightly dividing the word (**logos**) of truth.* **II Timothy 2:15 (KJV)**

The second Greek word that describes Scripture is *rhema*, referring to a word that is spoken and means "an utterance;" "a thing spoken, a word or saying of any kind, as command, report, a promise."[7]

A rhema is also a verse or portion of Scripture that the Holy Spirit quickens our attention to with application to a current situation or need. It is likened to an "eureka moment" or "oh now I get it" or "that word is just what I needed to hear."

---

[7] Strong's Concordance Greek rhema # 4487

The following passages of Scripture give biblical examples of the *rhema* of God:

- When the angel told Mary that she would have a child: *Mary said, Behold the handmaid of the Lord; be it unto me according to thy word. (rhema)* (**Luke 1:38, KJV**)
- Jesus said: *Man shall not live by bread alone, but by every word (rhema) that proceedeth out of the mouth of God.* (**Matthew 4:4, KJV**)
- Jesus also stated: *The words (rhema) that I speak unto you, they are spirit, and they are life.* (**John 6:63, KJV**)

Before we engage in the daily course of reading God's Word (*logos*), we need to pray and ask God to speak to us through His Word and to give us insight into it. The Holy Spirit can cause certain passages to stand out with significant meaning or application for our lives.

> *Every tomorrow has two handles. We can take hold of it by the handle of anxiety or by the hand of faith.*
>
> **Henry Ward Beecher**

These are the *rhemas* of Scripture that give us wisdom, comfort, direction and peace.

What's In It For Me?

So what does this all have to do with faith for the promises of God?

> *For the word (**logos**) of God is alive and powerful. It is sharper than the sharpest two-edged sword, cutting between soul and spirit, between joint and marrow. It exposes our innermost thoughts and desires*
> **Hebrew 4:12, NLT**

Many people are seeking for "a word," but the most consistent way that God gives us a word (*rhema*) is through The Word (*logos*).

Think about the logos and rhema like a fire in a fireplace.

The logos are the logs, the Holy Spirit is the flame and the rhema is the burning fire. As the Holy Spirit ignites the logs (logos), that Word becomes enflamed within our spirits and burns within us as a personal truth. As we experience challenges in our health, finances, family or just need a word of consolation or encouragement, the believer, armed with the logos and a rhema word, now has the confidence to boldly confess that rhema word. This produces the seed for "mountain moving faith" so we can **give our faith an assignment!**

Now the rhema fire needs to be stoked. The believer cannot allow difficulties to smother the fire of the rhema. Just as a natural fire needs to be stirred up to keep burning, so does the fire in our spirit. That is accomplished through: faith, confession, prayer, praise and worship, obedience to God's Word and other corresponding actions.

> *Faith does not operate in the realm of the possible. There is no glory for God in that which is humanly possible. Faith begins where man's power ends.*[8]
>
> **George Muller**

FAITH IS...

Putting another layer on the foundation of faith, let's delve into the familiar Scripture that defines faith found in **Hebrews 1:1**

Now faith is the substance of things hoped for, the evidence of things not seen. (**KJV**)

Now faith is confidence in what we hope for and assurance about what we do not see. (**NIV**)

Faith is the confidence that what we hope for will actually happen; it gives us assurance about things we cannot see. (**NLT**)

Faith assures us of things we expect and convinces us of the existence of things we cannot see.
(**GOD'S WORD TRANSLATION**)

Now faith is a well-grounded assurance of that for which we hope, and a conviction of the reality of things which we do not see. (**Weymouth**)

It is a well-known fact that when government agencies are training people to recognize counterfeit money, they do so by ingraining them with the characteristics of the real thing. The emphasis is on obtaining an intricate knowledge and familiarity with the genuine article so that when a counterfeit bill is presented to them, they recognize it readily, or if they have any doubts, they know how to test what has been presented to them.

So it is with the things of faith. We, as students of the Word, have to be able to recognize faith from hoping, wishing, foolishness, presumption or fantasy.

Merriam-Webster Dictionary[8] defines faith as: a strong belief or trust in someone or something; firm belief in something for which there is no proof.

---

[8] http://www.merriam-webster.com/dictionary/faith

Strong's Greek Concordance[9] cites the word for faith as *pistis,* which is defined as faith, belief, trust, confidence; fidelity, faithfulness.

The most threatening question that is being whispered in the hearts of many professing believers is probably never even voiced. That question simply asks, "What is real faith?"

There seems to be a popular connotation to the term faith that merely assigns it to mental attitude rather than spiritual conviction. The *real* message that is taught in Scripture has become weakened by humanistic concepts associated with positive thinking, mind power and other notions. There is a vast difference between a heart that has *faith in faith* and one that has *faith in God.*

> *Faith is energy, a force that empowers us to move, to take action, to accomplish some definite objective or purpose.*
>
> **Bishop Andrew JD Merritt**

My Faith is Taking Me Someplace[10]

---

[9] Strong's Concordance Greek pístis # 4102

A dynamic (dunamis) power without a specified direction or goal is dangerous and ineffective. Biblical faith has to have an **assignment**!

Jesus said, "I tell you the truth, if you had faith even as small as a mustard seed, <u>you could say</u> to this mountain, 'Move from here to there,' and it would move. Nothing would be impossible."
Matthew 17:20 (NLT, emphasis added)

Then Jesus told them, "I tell you the truth, if you have faith and don't doubt, you can do things like this and much more. <u>You can even say</u> to this mountain, 'May you be lifted up and thrown into the sea,' and it will happen.
Matthew 21:21, NLT (emphasis added)

And a woman was there who had been subject to bleeding for twelve years. She had suffered a great deal under the care of many doctors and had spent all she had, yet instead of getting better she grew worse. When she heard about Jesus, she came up behind him in the crowd and touched his cloak, <u>because she said,</u> <u>"If I just touch his clothes</u>, I will be healed."

---

[10]Merritt, Andrew, JD. My Faith is Taking Me Someplace. (1997). Creation House. Orlando, FL

Faith Is…

Immediately her bleeding stopped and she felt in her body that she was freed from her suffering.
He (Jesus) said to her, "Daughter, your faith has healed you. Go in peace and be freed from your suffering.
Mark 5:25-29; 34, NIV

FAITH IS NOT...

- *Just believing*

Belief is just mental assent or a feeling of being sure that something is true and while belief is one of the synonyms for faith, it is not enough. While faith is being unwaveringly convinced that something is true and within the will of God, even though it has not manifested in the natural realm—yet.

All of us have heard "only believe..." but believing a lie doesn't make it true (remember Santa Claus or the boogey man). Believing a lie, something that comes from our carnal desires, a perverted imagination or the whispers of satan is deception. Not only is it deceptive, but also dangerous as one expends their expectations, resources (time, money and talents), and spiritual reputation—often leading to despair; defeat; depression and a *decision of death*—"I will never believe God for anything else again!" (The tongue can bring death…Proverbs 18:21).

…all the ways that wickedness deceives those who are perishing. They perish because they refused to love the truth…
II Thessalonians 2:10b, NIV

• *Just a hoping and a wishing*

Hope is an anticipation or expectation that a desire will be fulfilled; a feeling of optimism. And while hope is a necessary component of faith; the chances that one's desires will be realized with only hope and no faith is hopeless. *Faith is the substance of things hoped for*—so you must have hope to give substance (reality) to your faith.

Hoped for…is future tensed; hope needs to be directed, it needs an object to reach for. But what do you do when the doctors say "there is no hope?" That is when we tap into the supernatural hope of God that is fostered through the Word of God.

…As it is written: I have made you the father of many nations.
He believed in God, *who gives life to the dead and* **calls things into existence that do not exist.**
He believed, hoping against hope, *so that he became the father of many nations according to what had been spoken:*
So will your descendants be.
Romans 4:17-18 Holman Christian Standard

Faith isn't like wishing upon a star; wishing on a wishbone or tossing coins in a wishing well. Wishing is the main ingredient of fairy tales and **Merriam-Webster** [11] defines a wish as "to have a desire for (as something *unattainable*). Nowhere in the entire 66 books of the Bible does God, the prophets or the red-letter words of Jesus tell us to wish for any of the promises of God.

For I know what I have planned for you,' says the LORD. 'I have plans to prosper you, not to harm you.
I have plans to give you a future filled with hope.
Jeremiah 29:11, NET BIBLE

---

[11] http://www.merriam-webster.com/dictionary/wish

• *Just faith alone*

How many times have we heard (*or said ourselves*), "I'm just waiting on God…" Well guess what—actually God is waiting on you!

So you see, faith by itself isn't enough. Unless it produces good deeds, it is dead and useless.
James 2:17, New Living Translation

Let's get one point clear: we can never work to earn or buy the blessings of God. However, there are "secondary works" that naturally result or flow out as a result of our faith. When you love someone, you naturally care about their well-being; you don't have to strenuously work at caring, you just do.

So it is with genuine faith—you are not working to get faith, but your faith has a by-product of works;

> *So also faith, if it is unaccompanied by obedience, has no life in it—so long as it stands alone.*
>
> **Weymouth Translation**

otherwise it is likened to a body without a spirit—dead and of no use.

Consider the following results of faith:

• *Salvation is a prerequisite*

You can't have genuine faith for God's promises of blessings, if you can't believe Him for the greatest blessing of all—the gift of salvation through faith in Jesus Christ as your Savior.

If you declare with your mouth that Jesus is Lord, and believe in your heart that God raised him from the dead, you will be saved.
Romans 10:9, NIV

• *Righteous living*

Being declared righteous in Jesus Christ through the finished work of The Cross is different than living righteously.

Being righteous means being right with God through the oneness of the human will with the will of God.

• *Obedience*

Obedience is non-negotiable.

Faith led Abraham to obey…
Hebrews 11:8

- *Forgiveness*

A hindrance to prayer is found in **Mark 11:25-26:**

And whenever you stand praying, if you have anything against anyone, forgive him, so that your Father in heaven will also forgive you your wrongdoing. But if you don't forgive, neither will your Father in heaven forgive your wrongdoing **(Holman Christian Standard)**

Prayer does not work without forgiveness

- *Love*

    As far as our relationship to Christ Jesus is concerned, it doesn't matter whether we are circumcised or not.
    But what matters is a faith that expresses itself through love
    Galatians 5:6, GOD'S WORD TRANSLATION

- *Prayer*

God does hear every prayer. Sometimes it may take longer than we expected or we did not get the answer we wanted; but even an "unanswered" prayer is an answer—no or not now!

*This is the confidence we have in approaching God:
that if we ask anything according to his will,
he hears us.
And if we know that he hears us—whatever we ask—
we know that we have what we asked of him.*
I John 5:14-15, NLT

• *Praise*

Praise means "to commend, to applaud or magnify."[12] When we praise God our focus is on Him as we lift our hearts above our troubles and current circumstances and enter into God's presence and power. We don't simply praise *after* we enter into the presence of the Lord, but we should praise in order to enter into His presence. The Scriptures say that God inhabits in the praises of His people (**Psalms 22:3**). Praise is a vehicle of faith that brings us into the presence and power of God!

---

[12] www.merriam-webster.com/dictionary/praise

- ## *Worship*

The word worship can be either a verb or noun. According to **Webster's Dictionary**[13], as a verb there are synonyms such as "esteem," "exalt," "revere," "glorify" and "respect." As a noun, synonyms are used such as, encompass adoration, veneration, devotion, supplication and invocation. When we obey the commandment to worship God, we are less apt to pervert our worship to the blessings that He has given us.

> *He (satan) said to Jesus, "I will give you all of these things if you will bow down and worship me!"*
> *Then Jesus said to him, "Go away, satan!*
> *For it is written, 'You must worship the Lord your God and serve only him."*
> **Matthew 4:9, ISV**

- ## *Thanksgiving*

We often hear that "David was a man after God's heart" because he was quick to repent and because he was a worshipper.

While that's true, another component of David's eminence was his heart-filled thanksgiving, as

---

[13] www.merriam-webster.com/dictionary/worship

evidenced by the countless expressions throughout the Psalms. We, like David, should have gratitude for the blessings of salvation, our daily provision, protection and the prosperity (well-being) yet to come.

The LORD is my strength and shield.
I trust him with all my heart.
He helps me, and my heart is filled with joy.
I burst out in songs of thanksgiving
Psalms 28:7, New Living Translation
(emphasis added)

With the heart a man believeth...
Romans 10:10

Faith is a function of the heart. If you believe negatively, you will eventually speak negative and you will reap negative in your life.

Faith-filled speech waters your faith and produces a harvest of a faith-full heart. Confession of the promises of God does not mean you have the faith for what you are saying. You must begin at the level where you can believe. Don't begin confessing for a million dollar mansion, when you can't believe God for rent for a $400 a month apartment.

A good person produces good things from the treasury of a good heart, and an evil person produces evil things from the treasury of an evil heart. What you say flows from what is in your heart.
Luke 6:45, New Living Translation

- ## *Sowing*

Remember the **Law of First Mention**?[14] Genesis, the book of beginnings, tells us that *everything produces after its own kind* (**v. 1:12**).

The Word of God is the seed that must be sown in order to reap a harvest. Other acts of faith include sowing a monetary or a material seed, or a deed of good works.

> *Faith makes things possible, not easy.*
> **Author Unknown**

- ## *Perseverance*

A harvest begins with the planting of a seed. The seed does not yield a harvest overnight or in a week. The Scripture tells us:

The earth produces the crops on its own.

---

[14] http://www.biblicalresearch.info

First a leaf blade pushes through, then the heads of wheat are formed, and finally the grain ripens.
Mark 4:28, NLT

GOD HAS DONE
ALL HE IS GOING TO DO.
HE HAS ALREADY GIVEN US
HIS SON JESUS SO THAT WE
WOULD HAVE AUTHORITY IN HIS
NAME, HIS BLOOD AND THE
FINISHED WORK OF THE CROSS;
HE GAVE HIS PROMISES SO THAT
WE WOULD HAVE SOMETHING
TO HOPE FOR;
AND HE GAVE HIS WORD SO
THAT WE WOULD HAVE
INSPIRATION, ILLUSTRATIONS
AND INSTRUCTIONS
OF HOW TO.

RAVENS WITH AN
ASSIGNMENT FROM GOD

When God gets ready to bless you, He can use anybody He chooses, including the unsaved or someone you normally would not have any association with. You may say, "Well what if they don't like me?" Who cares if they don't like you.

The king's heart is like streams of water. Both are under the LORD's control. He turned them in any direction he chooses.
Proverbs 21:1, GOD'S WORD TRANSLATION

The word heart in this Scripture is the Hebrew word *leb,* [15] and is defined as **mind, will, heart**. In other words, God can cause a person in authority

---

[15] Strong's Concordance Hebrew Leb # 3821

to have a change of heart or mind, or to change their will toward you and your situation.

God is Omnipotent (all-powerful) and can even use animals, fish, or birds to accomplish His purpose—remember the closed-mouth lions in the den with Daniel (**Daniel 6:22**); the fish that yachted Jonah in its belly for three days (**Jonah 2**); the tax-paying fish (**Matthew 17:27**); and the talking donkey (**Numbers 22:28**)?

Exploring this concept further, we will look closer into the miracle of provision recorded in **I Kings 17:2-6, NIV:**

Then the word of the Lord came to Elijah:
"Leave here, turn eastward and hide in the Kerith Ravine,
east of the Jordan. You will drink from the brook,
*and **I have directed the ravens to supply you with food there.**"*
So he did what the Lord had told him. He went to the Kerith Ravine, east of the Jordan, and stayed there.
The ravens brought him bread and meat in the morning and bread and meat in the evening,
and he drank from the brook. (emphasis added)

The KJV version of verse 4 reads:

*And it shall be, that thou shalt drink of the brook; and I
have **commanded** the ravens to feed thee there.
(emphasis added)*

God told Elijah that He **had already** commanded
the ravens. Elijah's responsibility was to **believe**
God and do the corresponding action by **obeying**
God and by going to Kerith Ravine, east of the
Jordan—the place where the provision was
awaiting him. The word **commanded or directed**
is the Hebrew word *tsavah*,[16] which means "to lay
charge (upon), give charge (to), to command, or
to order someone or something to do something."

Likewise use of this same word is found in **Amos
9:3b** when God commanded the serpents.

*Though they hide from my eyes at the bottom of the
sea, there I will **command** the serpent to bite them.
(emphasis added)*

The scriptures are abundantly clear that God can
use whatever means He chooses within His
creation to accomplish His ordained will.

---

[16] Strong's Concordance Hebrew Tsavah #6680

Let's take a closer look at the nature of "ravens." Whenever this passage of Scripture is preached, the expression often applied is that God used a "dirty bird." Interesting, **The National Geographic**[17] describes the raven as:

> Intelligent birds that are known as scavengers (*any animal that feeds on decaying organic matter*).

> Ravens are also effective hunters that sometimes use cooperative techniques. Teams of ravens have been known to hunt down game too large for a single bird.

> They also prey on eggs and nestlings of other birds, such as coastal seabirds, as well as rodents, grains, worms and insects.

> Ravens also dine on carrion (the dead and decaying flesh of an animal) and sometimes on human garbage.

Wow, the preachers are right—ravens are dirty birds!

Pay close attention. The Scripture did not say that Elijah fed the ravens, or feasted on ravens that he

---

[17] http://animals.nationalgeographic.com/animals/birds/raven

caught, nor does it say that he ravaged the nests of the ravens and stole the food that the birds had obtained for their babies.

The writings are clear: they brought him bread AND meat. Reviewing **The National Geographic** content, we see that ravens are hunters, not delivers. Not only did they *not* eat the food, but a coordinated team of ravens stayed on course day and night to feed the prophet. Commentators suggest that he was there at least a year.

Looking deeper, the word "bread" is the Hebrew word *lechem,*[18] which means food, especially bread, grain or fruit. The word "meat" is the Hebrew word *basar,*[19] meaning flesh (fresh flesh), thereby eliminating carrion or any dead flesh. Why is this a crucial point? Because Elijah was a law abiding Jew who understood the following laws:

---

[18] Strong's Concordance Hebrew Lechem # 3899
[19] Strong's Concordance Hebrew Basar # 1320

*These are the birds you are to detest and not eat because they are detestable: the eagle, the vulture, the black vulture, the red kite, any kind of black kite, any kind of **raven**…. (emphasis added)*
Leviticus 11:13-15

Or if a person touches anything ceremonially unclean—whether the carcasses of unclean wild animals or of unclean livestock or of unclean creatures that move along the ground—even though he is unaware of it, he has become unclean and is guilty.
Leviticus 5:2

Matthew Henry's Concise Commentary[20] notes, "God could have sent angels to minister to him; but he chose to show that He can serve His own purposes by the meanest creatures, as effectually as by the mightiest. Elijah seems to have continued thus above a year."

The Lord's Prayer, the model prayer, says, *"Give us today our daily bread"* (**Matthew 6:11**). However that word was truly fulfilled for Elijah, though they were spoken centuries apart as the ravens

---

[20] Concise Commentary on the Whole Bible by Matthew Henry
www.studylight.org/com

were faithful to their assignment to provide bread and meat for God's prophet day and night.

And God continued to *command* in order to ensure that His prophet ate. In **I Kings 17:9** we read that God told Elijah,

*Arise, get thee to Zarephath, which belongeth to Zidon, and dwell there: behold, **I have commanded** a widow woman there to sustain thee. (emphasis added)*

The word "command" in this verse is the same word *tsavah*; God commanded both the ravens and a widow to provide food to sustain one of His own. Elijah received

> *God can do more than man can understand*
>
> **Thomas 'a Kempis**
> **The Imitation of Christ**

his miracle because He believed and *obeyed God!*

Now faith is the substance of
things hoped for, the evidence
of things not seen.
Hebrews 11:1, KJV

Are you a faith man, a faith woman or a faith fake?

In other words, are you saying that you have something or you that believe something that hasn't manifested?

Evidence means proof. God wants you to be a recipient of the evidence or proof of your faith. I, reiterate: it is God's will that you receive. The fact that you are reading this book puts you in position to become a receiver; and if you receive the pure unadulterated, uncompromised Word of God, you *will* receive!

You don't have to take my word; the Bible has many Scriptures verifying that God wants us to receive:

- *Therefore I tell you, whatever you ask for in prayer, believe that you have received it, and it will be yours.* **(Mark 11:24, NIV)**
- *...For it gives your Father great happiness to give you the Kingdom.***(Luke 12:32, New Living Translation)**
- *...how much more shall your Father which is in heaven give good things to them that ask him?* **(Matthew 7:11, KJV)**

- *Seek the Kingdom of God above all else, and live righteously, and he will give you everything you need.* **(Matthew 6:33, NLT)**
- *Now without faith it is impossible to please God, for whoever comes to him must believe that he exists and that he rewards those who diligently search for him.* **(Hebrews 11:6, ISB)**
- *Ask, and it will be given to you; seek, and you will find; knock, and it will be opened to you.* **(Matthew 7:7, NASB)**
- *...Yet you don't have what you want because you don't ask God for it.* **(James 4:2, NLT)**

We have an obligation to use our faith *correctly,* by putting our confidence and total reliance in God. Subsequently, we will make a quality decision to abandon all works

> *If by faith you believe you are a receiver of the promises of God—then give God a shout of praise now!*

of the flesh, putting no confidence in any other flesh—no other person—only God. Not yourself, not your intelligence, not your abilities ... only God. If you pursue God, then He will reward you, and it will then become evident who gets rewarded and who is not rewarded. Understand this: if you do what God tells you to do, promotion is coming.

FOUR TYPES OF RECEIVERS IN THE BIBLE

- ## *The woman with the issue of blood.*

And a certain woman, which had an issue of blood twelve years, And had suffered many things of many physicians, and had spent all that she had, and was nothing bettered, but rather grew worse,
When she had heard of Jesus, came in the press behind, and touched his garment. For she said, If I may touch but his clothes, I shall be whole. And straightway the fountain of her blood was dried up; and she felt in her body that she was healed of that plague.
And Jesus, immediately knowing in himself that virtue had gone out of him, turned him about in the press, and said, Who touched my clothes?

And his disciples said unto him, Thou seest the multitude thronging thee, and sayest thou, Who touched me?
And he looked round about to see her that had done this thing. But the woman fearing and trembling, knowing what was done in her, came and fell down before him, and told him all the truth.
And he said unto her, Daughter, thy faith hath made thee whole; go in peace, and be whole of thy plague
Mark 5:25-34, KJV

A woman in the crowd had suffered for twelve years with constant bleeding, and she could find no cure. Coming up behind Jesus, she touched the fringe of his robe. Immediately, the bleeding stopped.
"Who touched me?" Jesus asked.
Everyone denied it, and Peter said, "Master, this whole crowd is pressing up against you." But Jesus said, "Someone deliberately touched me, for I felt healing power go out from me."…The whole crowd heard her explain why she had touched him and that she had been immediately healed. "Daughter," he said to her, "your faith has made you well. Go in peace."
Luke 8:43-48, NLT

Most of us have heard this story for years, but we have not really heard it in our inner man through the spirit of revelation.

Here is a woman who had every reason to complain; every reason to have a pity party; every reason to feel abandoned; every reason to not trust or to believe anything about the goodness of God. But the Bible says that when she **heard about Jesus...**

How do people hear about Jesus? They hear about Him from people who know Him and who have had an encounter with Him. They readily share their testimony and witness about the goodness of Jesus in their lives.

Evidently, it was being said in her community that Jesus was a healer. Just imagine that after twelve years of spending *all that she had,* and the doctors experimenting on her while she got no better, she could have given up and said, "I'm out of here." But she heard about Jesus...She heard about **The Word!**

So then faith cometh by hearing, and hearing by the word of God
Romans 10:17, KJV

Once she heard about Jesus, she got up and said *(audibly)*, if I could touch the hem of His garment.... Not just touch any part of His garment, *but* touch the hem; she was specific and designated her faith. **She gave her faith an assignment.**

You too, must give your faith an assignment—you cannot just say, "I have faith or I believe God"; you **must** give your faith an assignment. Designate your faith. Tell your faith what to do!

Let's look deeper into this woman's act of faith.

For she said within herself...

That is, she thought within herself, she reasoned the matter in her mind, she concluded upon it, and firmly believed it; being strongly impressed and influenced by the Spirit of God, and encouraged by instances of cures she had heard were performed by persons only touching him **(Gill's Exposition of the Entire Bible).**[21]

While she was making her declaration of faith and proceeding to approach Jesus, the scriptures say that a crowd of people began to gather and press in around Him.

> *And Jesus went with him; and a great crowd kept following Him and pressed Him from all sides [so as almost to suffocate Him].*
> **Mark 5:24, Amplified Bible**

In addition, a ruler of the Jewish synagogue had already approached Jesus to beseech Him on behalf of his twelve year old daughter who was at home, dying.

But woman with the issue of blood was fortified with a rhema word of faith. She was not distracted by the clamor of the surroundings or hindered by the Jewish laws that said she was considered unclean and should not have been out in the crowds of people **(Leviticus 15:19).**

---

[21] John Gill's Exposition of the Bible
www.biblestudytools.com/commentaries/gills-exposition-of the-bible

Her faith was assigned to just one thing — touching the hem of Jesus' garment and receiving her healing. But she received even more: "Go in peace" means not only quietness of soul but also total restoration!

• *Jarius, a Ruler of the Synagogue.*

And, behold, there cometh one of the rulers of the synagogue, Jairus by name; and when he saw him, he fell at his feet, And besought him greatly, saying, My little daughter lieth at the point of death:
I pray thee, come and lay thy hands on her,
that she may be healed;and she shall live.
And Jesus went with him; and much people followed him, and thronged him. While he yet spake, there came from the ruler of the synagogue's house certain which said,
Thy daughter is dead: why troublest thou the Master any further?
As soon as Jesus heard the word that was spoken, he saith unto the ruler of the synagogue, Be not afraid, only believe.
And he suffered no man to follow him, save Peter, and James, and John the brother of James. And he cometh to the house of the ruler of the synagogue, and seeth the

*tumult, and them that wept and wailed greatly. And
when he was come in, he saith unto them, Why make
ye this ado, and weep? the damsel is not dead, but
sleepeth.
And they laughed him to scorn.
But when he had put them all out, he taketh the father
and the mother of the damsel, and them that were with
him, and entereth in where the damsel was lying. And
he took the damsel by the hand, and said unto her,
Talitha cumi; which is, being interpreted,
Damsel, I say unto thee, arise.
And straightway the damsel arose, and walked;
for she was of the age of twelve years.
And they were astonished with a great astonishment.
And he charged them straitly that no man should
know it; and commanded that something should be
given her to eat.*
Mark 5:22-24; 35-43 (KJV)

The Amplified Version of verses 22-23 reads:

*Then one of the rulers of the synagogue came up,
Jairus by name; and seeing Him, he prostrated himself
at His feet
And begged Him earnestly, saying, My little daughter
is at the point of death.*

Come and lay Your hands on her, so that she may be healed and live.

Again in this account, we see this religious leader who in coming to Jesus believed and covenanted with himself, saying *(audibly)* that if Jesus would come and lay His hands on his dying daughter she would be healed and live.

Jesus said yes, I will come to your house, but at that very moment, an unseen woman touches Jesus, causing Him to stop, turn around, and to begin inquiry into who touched Him. Then the woman testified as to how she had assigned her faith for a healing.

Yet another distraction comes, as Jarius' servant came running up saying, don't bother Jesus — your twelve year old daughter is dead!

Overhearing but ignoring what they said,
Jesus said to the ruler of the synagogue,
Do not be seized with alarm and struck with fear;
only keep on believing
Mark 5:36, Amplified

In essence, Jesus was telling Jarius, stay focused on your faith assignment. Do not get distracted by what is going on around you, or the negative reports of other people. This is only the appearance of defeat. Remember your faith has an assignment, and *when I get to your house your daughter will be healed and will live!*

When Jesus arrived at Jarius' house the professional mourners were already there. Jesus inquired, "Why are you crying?" Answering, they said "because the damsel is dead." Jesus said, "No, she is only sleeping" and when they laughed at Jesus mockingly—He put them out of the room!

> *Countless Christians are talking a good talk about faith with no evidence, faking it.*
> *The world fakes it, until they make it—*
> *not the saints.*
> **Bishop Andrew JD Merritt**

Give Your Faith An Assignment

A word for you today:
Get rid of all negative, doubting,
double-minded people that are in your life.
Do like Jesus and put out all people
who don't see what you see;
who haven't heard what you heard;
don't feel what you feel; and
don't know what you know…
Get rid of them
Because this is about you and God!
Bishop Andrew JD Merritt

Now with an audience of those with like-minded faith, Peter, John, James, and the girl's father and mother, Jesus took the child by the hand and in his Aramaic tongue said "child arise."

And he put them all out, and took her by the hand,
and called, saying, Maid, arise.
So her spirit returned, and she got up at once. Then
Jesus directed that she be given something to eat.
Her parents were amazed, but he ordered them
not to tell anyone what had happened.
Luke 8:54-56, KJV/ISB

This father saw his faith assignment fulfilled because he was fortified with a rhema word from Jesus and so he did not lose hope.

Every day as Jarius watched his daughter grow to become a teenager, then a young lady and eventually marry and have children, his faith that God could do the impossible was solidified— Jarius' daughter was his faith extender!

- *The Centurion—The Captain of the Roman Army.*

When Jesus returned to Capernaum, a Roman officer came and pleaded with him, "Lord, my young servant lies in bed,
paralyzed and in terrible pain."
Jesus said, "I will come and heal him."
But the officer said, "Lord, I am not worthy to have you come into my home.
just say the word from where you are,
and my servant will be healed.
I know this because I am under the authority of my superior officers, and I have authority over my soldiers.
I only need to say,
'Go,' and they go, or 'Come,' and they come.
And if I say to my slaves, 'Do this,' they do it."

75

When Jesus heard this, he was amazed.
Turning to those who were following him, he said,
"I tell you the truth, I haven't seen faith like this in all
Israel!
Matthew 8:5-10, NLT

In this case, the centurion came to implore Jesus about his servant who was lying paralyzed at home, suffering terribly. *Jesus said, "I will come and heal him."* The centurion responded saying, *"Lord, I am not worthy that you should come under my roof: but speak the word only, and my servant shall be healed."* It is thought that the centurion felt unworthy to have Jesus come into his home; because as a Roman, he was considered to be a heathen (non-Jewish).

Then the centurion presented a tri-part message:

First, I am not worthy to have you come under the roof of my house.

Next, I understand authority. In fact, I am a man under authority, with soldiers under me. Saying to one, 'Go,' and he goes, and to another, 'Come,' and he comes, and to my servant, 'Do this,' and he does it." And I recognize that You are the only

One with authority in the Heavens, in the Earth, and under the Earth.

Last, and most important, he said, *I believe that standing right where You are*—that if You would just speak The Word only, my servant will be healed.

This Gentile soldier's faith was truly great. He had risen above the need of a sign, such as the touch of the garment's hem; or the laying on of hands. The authoritative Word of the Master would be enough.

This centurion's faith assignment impressed Jesus so much that He turned around to His disciples and said: *"I say unto you, I have not found so great faith, no, not in Israel"* (God's covenant people).

This is the kind of faith Jesus had been looking for. Even though he was not a Jew, the centurion had given his faith an assignment.

When Jesus heard these things, he marvelled at him, and turned him about, and said unto the people that followed him, I say unto you, I have not found so great faith, no, not in Israel. And they that were sent,

returning to the house, found the servant whole that had been sick.
Luke 7:9-10, KJV

The New Living Translation says it this way:

Then Jesus said to the Roman officer, "Go back home. Because you believed, it has happened."
And the young servant was healed that same hour.
Matthew 8:13

The Roman Centurion, like the woman with the issue of blood and Jarius, and countless others, saw his faith assignment accomplished.

• *Blind Bartimaeus*

Take note of this account as it is recorded in **Mark 10:46-52, (CEV):**

Jesus and his disciples went to Jericho. And as they were leaving, they were followed by a large crowd. A blind beggar by the name of Bartimaeus son of Timaeus was sitting beside the road.
When he heard that it was Jesus from Nazareth, he shouted,
"Jesus, Son of David, have pity on me!"

Many people told the man to stop, but he shouted even
louder,
"Son of David, have pity on me!"
Jesus stopped and said, "Call him over!"
They called out to the blind man and said, "Don't be
afraid! Come on! He is calling for you." The man
threw off his coat as he jumped up and ran to Jesus.
Jesus asked, "What do you want me to do for you?"
The blind man answered, "Master, I want to
see!"Jesus told him,
"You may go. Your eyes are healed because of your
faith."
Right away the man could see, and he went down the
road with Jesus.

Now, let's look at this character known as blind Bartimaeus a little closer. This man was not only known for being blind, but also for being one who sat by the highway begging for money. As part of his attire, he wore a beggar's cloak, *the official uniform of beggars.* This coat served a dual purpose in a beggar's life; it was their identity in the daytime and their comfort at night as they lay upon it as a pallet.

But as he sat by the road daily, Bartimaeus had opportunity to hear all of the latest gossip and news of the city. He also heard that Jesus healed the sick, raised the dead, cast out demonic spirits, opened deaf ears and gave sight to the blind. Surely, as he heard the testimonial accounts of the miracles performed by Jesus, his faith grew and he *said* within himself, when Jesus comes by, "I am going to get my sight!"

Notice the Scripture don't show him calling out for help to anyone; but when he *heard* Jesus was at hand, he called out to Jesus *in faith*...the people rebuked him and told him to be quiet! But he raised his voice even louder above the noise of the naysayers, saying, "Son of David, have mercy on me!" And when Jesus heard him He stopped...

Jesus said come here!

The blind man threw off his coat, jumped up, and went to Jesus.
Mark 10:50 (NLT)

This blind beggar threw off his coat—his long held identity as a beggar. He jumped up and came to Jesus—still blind, but no longer *seeing* himself as a beggar—as an act of his faith. Then the story takes an unusual twist as Jesus asks him, "What do you want Me to do for you?" **WHAT?**

To the casual onlooker, it would seem obvious what Bartimaeus wanted. But Jesus wanted to know if Bartimaeus had **given his faith an assignment.**

This man devoid of sight, but great in faith boldly proclaimed, I want to see! *And Jesus said to him, "Go, for your faith has healed you." Instantly the man could see, and he followed Jesus down the road.*
Mark 10:52, NLT

Within a matter of minutes Bartimaeus' entire life was different. He threw off the beggar's cloak and put on the garment of praise. He went from begging to discipleship, and from just sitting on the side of the road to following Jesus on that same road. When God blesses you, life as you know it will never be the same.

A DISCOURSE ON FAITH

The following are excerpts from "The Act of Faith," a sermon delivered by Bishop Merritt at Straight Gate International Church, in Detroit Michigan on February 2, 2014.

- Faith is a fact.
- Faith is active and so cannot lay dormant.
- Faith is present tense.
- Your faith must be solid and able to stand the wiles of the enemy; the attacks of the enemy.
- Faith is not just something that you read about, then you just start walking in it—not realizing that every act of faith must be tested.
- Every rhema word of faith that God gives you will be challenged by satan.

- Faith never considers the consequences. Faith never sits down and counts the costs and says that can't happen for me—it eliminates all of that because faith goes beyond the natural; it is an act or a walk into the supernatural.

- If you are not anchored in and tied in to Jesus—you are not going to be able to stand the testing of your faith.

- Nobody can live your faith but you.

- The woman who had been bleeding for twelve years said, "IF I may touch His garment, I shall be whole"—that was her declaration of faith.

- Jesus said, "Woman thy faith has made thee whole"...not her touch **(Matthew 9:22/Mark 5:34),** it was her faith that gave birth to the touch.

- People who reach out are the only ones who come away with something; they are the only ones who make something happen; some people just sit down with their arms folded saying, "Nothing good ever happens for me." No, *nothing ever will happen* for them because faith is an act!

- If I can believe it, and I need it and it doesn't already exists in this Earth, then God can create it.
- Consider the story of the man who was born blind. God spit into the dirt to make clay, put it on the man's eyes (making him doubly blind) and told him to wash. Now how do you tell a blind man to go to wash? And not just in any pool, but the pool of Siloam. After the man went to do what Jesus said and washed, he then had eyes that he could see with.
- Don't allow anybody to put you in a mold and say this can't be done. God specializes in things that are impossible for man.
- There is nothing too difficult or hard for God, and if you can believe, you can receive the impossible!
- You can live an extraordinary life with God!
- Faith opens every door. Let me tell you a secret that is in the Bible. Jesus has the keys to the door and He said, If I lock the door, I will keep your enemies out...and if the enemy is trying to keep you out, because Jesus has the keys, He said I will open that door for you.

- Sometimes we run ahead of God. This is presumption on our part and is a sin. A good example is Abraham and Sarah agreeing to raise up an Ishmael. Behaving this way is going to result in extra work on our part, so that we learn the lesson to not be presumptuous and move ahead of God's timing.

- When God tells you to do something it is guaranteed.

- When a man releases his sperm to impregnate his wife, there are millions of sperm released, but there is only one that has the "push" of God to get pass all the other sperm to get to that egg.

- You will be surprised at what God does.

- If God told you to do something, it is done! It is not just possible, it is already done!

- Faith is the inward operation of the divine power that dwells in the broken and contrite heart; it doesn't just dwell anywhere, it only dwells in the broken and contrite heart. *The sacrifices of God are a broken spirit: a broken and a contrite heart, O God, thou wilt not despise* **(Psalms 51:17, KJV).**

- An unbroken heart is resistant and has its own agenda. It is undisciplined, and unsubmissive. You cannot break your own heart and you cannot cause your heart to be contrite; but God can. Obedience is non-negotiable.
- Faith is a divine act.
- Faith is the hand of God; faith is the power of God; faith never fears; faith lives in the midst of the greatest conflicts.
- Faith is God in the soul.
- God operates by His Son and transforms the supernatural into the natural.
- If God tells you to go, just go, He will order your steps.
- You cannot live by faith until you are righteous.
- If you are living unrighteously, you have eliminated yourself from the God's divine interventions and from God's power source, the Holy Ghost on the inside of you—the supernatural, the miracle working power of God! (**Psalms 34:17**).
- So in the midst of your trials and temptations, in the midst of the enemy coming in like a flood, the Lord says keep

walking, maintain your righteousness and your holiness, and I will lift up a standard that the enemy cannot overcome. Be still and I will fight your battles.

- Leave yourself in the hands of God, this (The Word of God) is supposed to work, because if it doesn't that would make God a liar and we know that God cannot lie (**Isaiah 55:11**); so if things are not working, I must conclude that the problem is me.

- If God gives you an assignment, you submit to do it!

- It is best to say yes to God, not the second time, but the first time. Because it is going to be God's way or the highway.

- If God is in you, then God is with you; and if God is in you and with you then God is for you. And if God is for you, then who in the world can be against you?
  When the enemy comes against you, he comes against God.

- Countless Christians are talking a good talk about faith with no evidence, just faking it. The world fakes it, until they make it—not the saints.

MY FINAL THOUGHTS

Some of you may be thinking, all of this "**Give Your Faith An Assignment**" stuff sounds great but does this only work when I have a desperate case like Elijah or Jarius? The answer is a resounding **NO**!

The Bible has given us an ingenuous promise that is repeated at least four times.

- May He give you the *desire of your heart* and make all your plans succeed.
  Psalms 20:4 (NIV)
- For You have given him his *heart's desire*; You have withheld nothing he requested (**Psalms 21:2, NLT**)
- Take delight in the LORD, and He will give you the *desires of your heart* (**Psalms 37:4, NIV**)

- He grants *the desires* of those who fear (reverence, honor) Him; He hears their cries for help and rescues them **(Psalms 145:19, NLT)**

Why would God inspire men to write the same idea or concept over and over again? Because ideas are often repeated in the Bible in different contexts to get you to think more about their meaning. Sometimes we see things differently when they are presented in a different light or context. We see this often in the books of **Psalms** and **Proverbs** where the same idea is mentioned again and again with a slightly different wording. But the purpose remains the same: to get the reader or the believer to ponder, and through repetition to know this *is* the will of God for his or her life.

Now you know assuredly that it is God's will to not just grant you a healing or a meal, but it is also His will to grant you the desires of your heart.

Let's look at a biblical example of a heart's desire.

My Final Thoughts

On the third day a wedding took place at Cana in Galilee.

Jesus' mother was there, and Jesus and his disciples had also been invited to the wedding. When the wine was gone,

Jesus' mother said to him, "They have no more wine."

"Woman, why do you involve me?" Jesus replied.

"My hour has not yet come."

His mother said to the servants, "Do whatever he tells you."

Nearby stood six stone water jars, the kind used by the Jews for ceremonial washing, each holding from twenty to thirty gallons.

Jesus said to the servants, "Fill the jars with water"; so they filled them to the brim.

He told them, "Now draw some out and take it to the master of the banquet."

They did so, and the master of the banquet tasted the water that had been turned into wine. He did not realize where it had come from, though the servants who had drawn the water knew.

Then he called the bridegroom aside and said, "Everyone brings out the choice wine first and then the cheaper wine after the guests have had too much to drink; but you have saved the best till now."

What Jesus did here in Cana of Galilee was the first of the signs through which he revealed his glory; and his disciples believed in him.

John 2:1-11, NIV

For most of us, running out of wine at a wedding is not an indication for us to seek a miracle from Jesus. However, the cultural milieu suggests that the couple getting married was somehow related to Mary; possibly a close relative because she took such an interest in the fact that they had run out of wine.

During this period of time, wedding feasts lasted anywhere from seven to fourteen days thus accounting for the exhaustion of the supply of wine. This would have proven to be a source of great embarrassment and humiliation for the family as they obviously either miscalculated the needs for the celebration (this was only the third day) or they did not have the financial resources to supply what was needed.

Verse **3** says, *"When the wine ran out, the mother of Jesus said to Him, 'They have no wine.'"* (**NASB**) This comment indicates there was an obvious desire for more wine. She now **gave her faith an**

assignment and said to the servants,*"Whatever He tells you to do, do it."* This wasn't Jesus' wedding and He didn't seem to be concerned about the lack of wine. But His mother desired that there be more wine for the remainder of the feast.

It is thought that these six jars filled with water yielded more than 134 gallons of high quality wine![22] Not only did the governor of the feast not know where the wine came from; apparently the bridegroom did not know that Jesus Himself was working a miracle on his behalf. The bridegroom experienced a miracle because of the **faith assignment** of another person—*Selah.*

...and the master of the banquet tasted the water that had been turned into wine. He did not realize where it had come from, though the servants who had drawn the water knew. Then he called the bridegroom aside.

(v. **9**)

Understand that a person cannot use their faith to cause something that is against your will or desires. The gourmet vino was something that the bridegroom would have had a desire for in that

---

[22] The Pulpit Commentaries www.studylight.org/com/tpc

particular situation. When I speak of using your faith for the desires of your heart, I am not talking about foolishness, presumption or unrighteousness. The desires of your heart must be in accord with the will and the Word of God in order for your **faith assignment** to be effective— remember the *conditional* promises?

Give Your Faith An Assignment is a guide to facilitate you in purposefully using your God-given authority and assigning it to specific, deliberate, intentional needs and desires.

Faith is a phenomenal gift from God that is to be used for more than securing our salvation. Faith is the currency of exchange for the things of God; and we can get nothing from God outside of faith.

> *I want everything*
> *God has intended*
> *for me to have.*
> **Bishop Andrew JD**
> **Merritt**

Often times we hear people say, "Try God." But you don't "Try God"; you either believe Him or you don't.

The scriptures are rich with examples of people, who have assigned their faith to get their needs and desires met and to intercede correspondingly for others. Remember, the ways of God are unchangeable; they are the same today as they were yesterday.

In essence, in order to **give your faith an assignment**, you have to be single-minded; the Bible tells us that *a double-minded man is unstable in all his ways* (**James 1:8, KJV**).

You have to draw an irreversible faith line; determining to never go back to fear, doubt and unbelief and to lay ahold of what God has promised you!

TESTIMONIES

Over the years, I have received hundreds of testimonies from people who have heard and applied the principles presented in **Give Your Faith An Assignment.**

The next few pages will highlight just a few of these instances. Each testimony is un-edited, verified as true, and well supported with the relevant documentation.

The blessings cover the gamut from healings, to financial break-throughs, to miracle children for infertile couples, and the prevention of a suicide—to name a few!

You too can **give your faith an assignment!**

Dear Bishop Merritt:

I wanted to take the time to say thank you. I attended today's third service and God directed you to pray for me at length. Although I know that all praise and glory be given to God, I want to acknowledge my gratitude to you as well. I specifically want to thank you for all the time and sacrifice it takes to prepare to provide for the spiritual needs of people like me. If not for your obedience and dedication to God and His Word, you would not be in a place to hear His voice and in turn, reach out to someone like me.

I am a fifty year old man, who, at times, has seemed to have everything by the world's standards—but at the same time, be completely empty inside. Today you instructed people in our service to write down on a piece of paper those things that seemed dead and hopeless. I wrote down "hopes, dreams, vision and my business." It's unlike me to jump up and respond to such a call, but in my spirit I know I had to.

I'd like to tell you my story...but I'd never make it back to the six 'o clock service on time tonight! I'll just say that circumstances in my life had become so disappointing within the last few years that I had even considered suicide and some low points, even though I have a loving wife and son.

Today, as you continued to pray with different individuals throughout the congregation, I purposely closed my eyes and prayed silently to God that if there was a way for you to see me in the great sea of people—in order to pray with me and for me, you would do so. I never opened my eyes; I simply kept praying and focused on God.

When you touched me, I actually was startled. It wasn't until my wife and I were on our way home that she told me how you came straight through the center aisle towards me like an anointed man on a mission. Once I finally looked up at you after you had prayed for several minutes with me, all I could muster in words were, "I've been broken for so long." You said, "You are whole now..."

I'll never forget those words or the face from which the words came. I will lift you up in prayer every day that God will bless you and use you to touch others like you've touched me. It has been my prayer for the last ten months that the second half of my life will be able to fulfill the purpose for which God created me. I continue to cry out for God's wisdom and direction in order to fulfill that purpose. Again, I want to thank you for your sacrifice and prayer that place you in a position to hear God and see me.

With much respect,
Michael

* * * * *

From: Gwendolyn H. S

Subject: Greetings from Mitchellville, Maryland

Bishop Merritt,

After the passing of my mother in May/2014, I returned home (Detroit) in June to handle the task of packing her earthly possessions. While home, I had lunch with a dear friend of the family who is a faithful member (Karen D.) of Straight Gate International Church. As a loving gesture, Karen blessed me with a copy of your book "My Faith is Taking Me Someplace." Needless to say...after reading your book I had to Google your name to satisfy the burning question; "who is this CAT? (she smiles), not aware of what was really getting ready to happen in my life. What I came across after researching your name was the unadulterated, uncompromising word of God through **FYF.TV.** Bishop, it would take up too much of your time to elaborate on my entire testimony so I will be brief. I'm on fire for our Savior Jesus Christ. The Jesus in you has altered my faith, now I no longer have dry bones because the Holy Spirit resides in me. The cobwebs have been dusted off and now I worship God in spirit and in truth, My eyes are opened. God has used you to penetrate my heart and now I'm praising God for the renewal of my mind. I thank God for your teaching and your connection with Dr. Bill Winston. The messages help so many learn the truth! The word says in Hosea 4:6; My people are destroyed for lack of knowledge.

Fast forward...I'm coming home for Thanksgiving, and my family and I look forward to seeing and meeting you on Sunday, November 30, 2014, at the 10.00 am service. So much has happened since reading your book and becoming a partner with **FYF.TV.** I walk with authority and my faith has equipped me to launch (December 1, 2014) a new business. Hebrew 11:1, Bishop, you showed me, not yesterday, nor tomorrow, or next week but, "NOW" faith is the substance of things

Give Your Faith An Assignment

hoped for, the evidence of things not seen. The Holy Spirit has guided me through the entire process. I no longer lean on my own understanding. Glory to God.

Bishop, I have a gift for you that will explain the impact that your series on 7 Days of Faith Conference had on my life. This is the season of Thanksgiving, and I am thankful that God chose you, a son of God, for me, a son of God.

Warm Regards to Sister Vickie and your entire family.

Sincerely,
Gwen S.

* * * * *

Job Testimony
Malikah G.
I am currently the manager in metro Detroit, MI for Kaplan Test prep which helps students get into graduate schools. I have been with the company for 1 year and 5 months. Earlier this year they announced that they are transitioning to a leaner way of doing business and will go from having around 140 managers across the country,

down to about 40. People were going to lose their jobs. For Michigan, there are 3 managers (including me) and 1 director (who is my current boss). They were going down to 1 manager for the entire state. Not only was I competing with my colleagues and boss for the new job, but others outside of Michigan could apply as well because it is a virtual/ work from home position. My husband and I prayed after the announcement and trusted God's will for me. We told God we trust Him to take care of us because we are tithers. I applied for the new position and had my interview. I had peace the entire time. Shortly after my interview, God showed me in a dream that the new job was His will. About 3 weeks later, I was offered the position of Graduate Programs Manager for the entire State of Michigan. I beat out my Director, colleagues, and all others that applied. I now manage over $3 million dollars in business a year. I make more money and now work from home 95% of the time. What a mighty God we serve!

* * * * *

Testimony from Inmates of Milan Prison

On December 12, Bishop Merritt ministered at Milan Federal Prison. His message was taken from Matthew 14:22-23, and the inmates were told that we serve God by "faith." On the command of Jesus "To Come," Peter walked on the water by faith until the wind and waves began to get rough and his response was "LORD, SAVE ME!" God gave Bishop Merritt a Prophetic word and instructed the inmates to "CALL YOUR LAWYER TOMORROW" the one who represented you before the judge who sentenced you. Tell your lawyer to call the Judge and tell HIM to "SAVE ME."

During the following months, the prison ministry team from the Straight Gate International Church received testimonies from the men at Milan Federal Prison. These are the three: one inmate had two prior counts against him and a $75,000.00 bond besides the actual charge that landed him in this institution. When he heard the message, which Bishop Merritt ministered, he didn't have a lawyer so he wrote a letter to Jesus saying, "Save Me." A few days later, another inmate approached him with the name of an attorney.

The attorney took the case, contacted the court, the counts were dropped and the bond money returned. He then became in position for an earlier release.

Another inmate had not talked to his attorney in years, when he called him, he was shocked that the attorney answered the phone. He told him what Bishop Merritt had instructed "save me." Shortly after, he received three letters informing him that "five years" had been taken off his sentence, putting him in position to be released into a halfway house.

And thirdly, another inmate from a foreign country had not seen his wife in over twenty years, while she was in the process of coming to America to see him her visa was denied. This man heard the message and knew Jesus would "save them." The U.S, Ambassador in their country was called and the visa granted and the wife was now on U.S. soil.

* * * * *

On Sunday, January 13, 1991, Bishop Merritt declared to the congregation of Straight Gate Church that "it will be a short war!"

The Gulf War (Desert Storm) began on Wednesday, January 16, 1991 at 7 pm (EST) and ended 42 days later on Thursday, February 28th.

Bishop Merritt prophesied that Senator Barack Obama will be "President of the United States of America" several months before he received the democratic nomination!

He received the nomination in August 2008.

Barack Obama was sworn in as the 44th president of the United States on January 20, 2009.

ABOUT THE AUTHOR

Andrew Merritt is a bishop, author, city statesman, business owner and visionary leader. In 1978, he and his wife Pastor Viveca Merritt founded the Straight Gate International Church in Detroit, Michigan. The church has experienced phenomenal growth—from three members in 1978 to eight church moves to serve the needs of the emerging congregation of more than 6,000 today.

A respected minister and community leader, Bishop Merritt has prayed with Presidents Clinton and G. W. Bush, as well as, Michigan's former Governor Jennifer Granholm and former mayors of the City of Detroit.

Bishop Merritt also served as co-chair of the International Mandela Freedom Tour to the City of Detroit, 1990.

In 2004, Bishop and his wife launched the international annual conference, One In Worship, that gathers thousands from the body of Christ in one accord for the sole purpose of praise and worship.

The Merritt's family-managed record company, M&M Entertainment and Bajada Records, has produced numerous gospel and inspirational recordings, as well as Stellar-nominated hits.

A family-focused minister, Bishop is the proud father of six children, nine grandchildren and one great-grandchild. He has also authored six other books. He is considered a Pastor of Pastors. Bishops and pastors nationwide acknowledge Bishop Merritt as their spiritual father and covering in the ministry because of the anointing on his life.